Daddy
Saved the Day

Angela Shelf Medearis
Illustrated by Michelle Mills

Rigby

Executive Editor: Lynelle H. Morgenthaler
Senior Designer: Tom Sjoerdsma

04 03 02 01 00 99
10 9 8 7 6 5 4 3 2 1

Printed in Singapore

ISBN 0-7635-5701-3

Everyone came from near and far for our family reunion, just like they always do. We took picture after picture, all huddled close in front of Grandma Angeline's house. It felt like a giant hug. Uncle Arthur kept saying, "Okay, now everybody smile!" And we did, because we were so happy to be together.

Daddy Howard was the oldest person there, and three-year-old Cousin Jessica was the youngest. The relatives passed her from hand to hand as if she were a living doll.

The sun was blazing hot, just like it always is
when it's summertime in Texas, but we played
basketball anyway. Cousin Joey, Uncle Howard,
Cousin Kennie Ray, and Cousin Michael tried
some fancy moves when they threw the ball into
the basket. After the game, everybody swam in
the chilly water of Grandma's pool to cool off.

5

Like always, we had barbecue at the family reunion. The menfolk tended to the barbecue pit. They talked and laughed and teased each other about who can cook the best. The smell of hickory smoke filled the air, tickled our noses, and teased our stomachs. When Grandma Angeline told us it was time to eat, we scrambled inside.

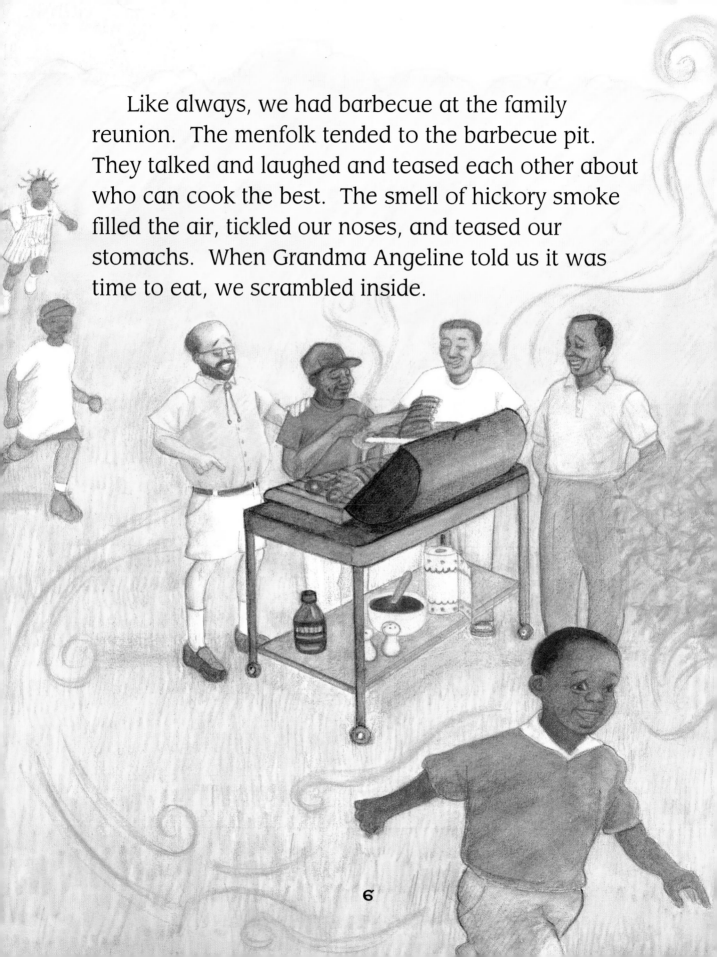

At one end of the table stood a huge bowl of creamy potato salad sprinkled with red paprika and a container of tangy purple coleslaw. Cousin Pat's fruit salad was so colorful it looked like it was dressed up for the reunion. Pans of hot buttered rolls, crocks of Aunt Angela's delicious baked beans, and platters of crispy ribs and juicy smoked chicken took up the rest of the table. Soon everyone's face was covered with a shiny layer of barbecue sauce.

Then Grandma started talking about dessert, just like she always does. She had made so many layer cakes that they crowded each other on the cabinet. Cousin Marcy ate German chocolate cake with a Texas-sized scoop of ice cream, even though she said she was on a diet. I had some too, but I had to eat it slow so that my stomach could make room for it among all that barbecued chicken and baked beans.

We were so full we couldn't even swat at the flies. They buzzed around us as if they were putting on a summertime symphony.

Then Daddy said, "Let's have a talent show," just like he always does. We all went into the living room. The adults sat on the couches, and the children sat on the floor. Aunt Sandra sang and played hymns on the piano. It wasn't long before the adults were shouting like it was a Sunday morning church service. Aunt Icie waved her hands in the air, just like she always does when the music moves her. My other relatives sang out the last lines of Aunt Sandra's song and clapped their hands.

Then Aunt Liz, Aunt Joyce, Uncle Leon, Aunt Trudy, and Aunt Immogene sang their songs. They closed their eyes, threw back their heads, and swayed to the rhythm.

Then someone asked Aunt Angela to tell a story. Now I love hearing Aunt Angela's stories during the daytime, but they come back to haunt me at night. The moonlight makes spooky shapes on my wall like the ghosts in her stories. My jacket and cap look like the creatures she whispers about. After hearing one of Aunt Angela's stories, I usually have to sleep with the light on.

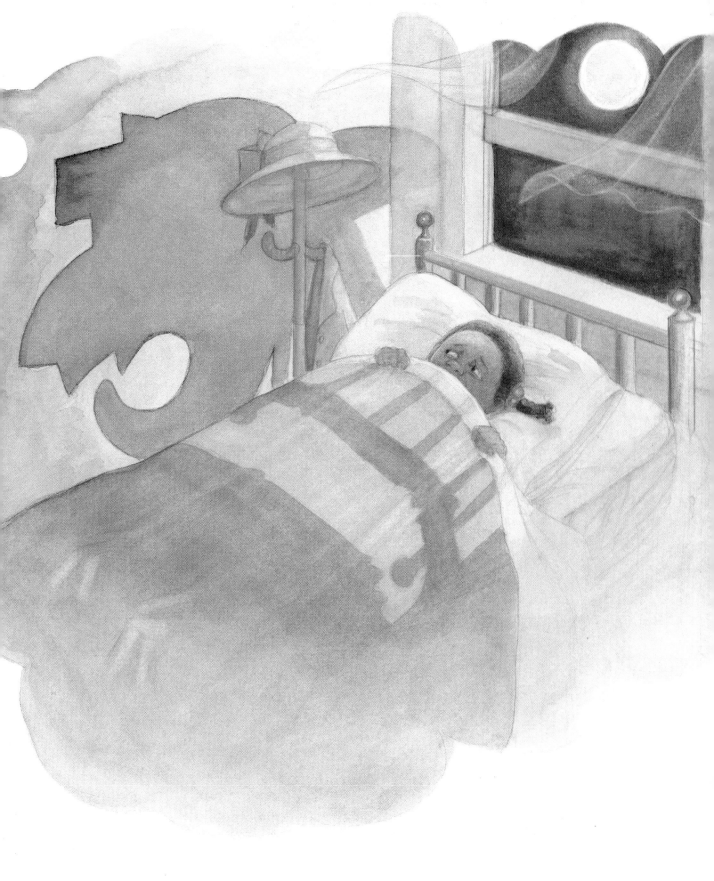

Wouldn't you know it! Aunt Angela decided to tell us about a haunted house! She swung right into her story—twisting her lips, hunching her shoulders, and widening her eyes as she described creepy creatures and monstrous men. She curled her fingers and whipped her head from side to side as she spun her terrible tale. She peered out through her long braids as if through thick, black vines, while whispering in a scratchy voice.

During the scariest part, I forgot to breathe. I felt light-headed, and my heart was beating so loud I was sure that Cousin Cameron and Cousin Courtney could hear it. Aunt Angela made her voice rumble like distant thunder, and then she screamed so loud the adults jumped in their seats and the children clung to each other.

She finished her story with a cackling laugh. The sun had disappeared, and the night covered everything like a thick, black blanket. We were too spooked to speak or move. Then Daddy saved the day.

17

Daddy sat down at the piano and began pounding the keys. Aunt Florine's eyes sparkled, and the children sat up straight. Daddy's boogie-woogie music floated from the piano into our feet. Everyone began to dance. With flying feet and snapping fingers, old and young alike danced around Grandma's living room.

Uncle Michael was supposed to videotape the whole event, but Daddy's boogie-woogie made him forget about the camera and begin twirling around with little Cousin Anysa.

Daddy's hands flew up and down the keyboard, pounding the white keys and tickling the black ones. His feet tapped out the time as he bit his lip with concentration. He played and we danced till all of us were covered with sweat and couldn't catch our breath.

When the music stopped, the adults collapsed on the sofa and draped themselves across chairs. The children lay on the floor in a heap like a bunch of sleepy puppies.